AMERICAN
MILITARY AIRCRAFT

AMERICAN
MILITARY AIRCRAFT

GALLERY BOOKS
An Imprint of W. H. Smith Publishers Inc.

112·Madison Avenue New York NY 10016

THE IMAGE BANK®

111 Fifth Avenue New York NY 10003

First published in 1988 in New York by Gallery
Books, an imprint of W.H. Smith Publishers Inc.,
112 Madison Avenue, New York, N.Y. 10016

ISBN 0-8317-6913-0

For rights information about the photographs in
this book please contact:

The Image Bank
111 Fifth Avenue, New York, N.Y. 10003

Manufactured in Singapore

Produced by Robert M. Tod
Art Direction and Design by Mark Weinberg
Assistant Art Direction by Dana Shimizu Lee
Written by Bill Gunston
Edited by Sheila Buff
Photo Research: David Clark
Editorial Assistance: Elizabeth Loonan

Contents

Collected in this book are portraits of the chief types of airplanes and helicopters used by the United States fighting forces—the Air Force, Navy, Marine Corps and Army. The United States has plenty of air power. The Navy alone has often been described as "the world's fourth-largest air force," and it is not long since the US Army had more military helicopters than all the rest of the world combined.

But American airpower is not just quantity: we like to think the equipment pictured in this book is the best in the world. It is said that imitation is the sincerest form of flattery, and the aircraft designers of the Soviet Union have obviously been very strongly influenced by the latest generation of American warplanes. The Sukhoi 24 "Fencer" is pretty much a Russian edition of the USAF's General Dynamics F-111. The same design team's Su-25 "Frogfoot" was obviously inspired by the USAF's A-10, and in fact looks even more like the Northrop A-9A (the plane the USAF *didn't* buy!). And you have only to glance at the latest MiG fighter, the MiG-29 "Fulcrum," to see its resemblance to the USAF's top fighter, the McDonnell Douglas F-15 Eagle.

America can be proud of its warplanes. They are the result of the best efforts of the world's most powerful aerospace companies, who—though they take a keen interest in what their rivals do—would never dream of copying anyone. Time after time US design teams have thrust ahead into previously unknown areas of technology. They were first in the world to build giant jet bombers with wings and tail swept back to fly at close to the speed of sound. They were the first to build an intercontinental ballistic missile, and the first to develop such a missile that could be fired from a submerged submarine. They pioneered successful long-range jetliners—to such good effect that until recently almost every airline jet in the world was American. They were the first to build armed helicopters, menacing machines which, despite being helicopters, can kill the thickest-skinned tank. They were the pioneers of the high-flying radar station, which can "see" more than 230 miles in all directions. They were the first to build an attack airplane that can fly at close to the speed of sound only just above the ground, even in mountains, at night or in cloud, in order to come in under the defending radar beams and hit the enemy not only with precision but also with surprise. They were the first to build gigantic transports that can fly to the other side of the world carrying virtually everything needed by any fighting force. And, of course, no nation has anything remotely resembling the mighty seagoing air power of the United States Navy, which can rule the skies and the sea, and to a considerable degree can also rule the land, anywhere on earth.

Along with this, US airpower is popular. It has never been used to oppress but to keep the peace. If you go to Rio de Janeiro, Melbourne, Tokyo or London you will find books, magazines and plastic kits stuffed full of American warplanes, and especially the "sexy" fighters. These are the airplanes that most excite boys—and older boys—the world over. They put on brilliant performances at airshows, making seemingly impossible maneuvers with white vapors streaming from their wings. Many are battle-proven, often while wearing the colors of friendly nations.

This mention of colors leads to what is visually the only thing to regret about modern American warplanes. How do you best paint a warplane? In World War I, in 1917-18, the Allied airplanes went into action painted a somber olive drab (though admittedly the crack squadrons and pilots embellished their airplanes with unit badges or individual artistry reflecting the pride they felt in their squadron or a natural wish to "customize" their own airplane). In contrast, the enemy German fighters were painted in the most striking and flamboyant manner possible, with brilliant stripes and checkerboard markings, giant eagles and serpents, and whatever the pilot thought would intimidate the enemy.

The dichotomy between the need for somber camouflage and the wish to paint one's airplane in a bold way that proclaims "we're the greatest" has continued right up to the present time. One saw it in the tail markings of USAF F-15s and even more strikingly in the superb paint schemes of the Navy F-14 Tomcats. Today, however, the hottest ships in the sky are all being repainted in ways that will make them as inconspicuous as possible. Almost every combat airplane is now painted all over in various shades of gray, which in most conditions of sunlight, cloudscape and earth background are reckoned to make the airplane as difficult to see as possible. Even the US national insignia, formerly boldly emblazoned in red, white and blue, is now merely outlined in dark gray.

As for the non-combatant transports, air-refueling tankers and similar airplanes, these used to be brilliant white and shiny metal, with multicolored markings. Today all have been repainted in a more warlike camouflage of three shades of dark green. This livery is called Europe 1, but is not confined to airplanes of USAFE (US Air Forces Europe). As for the unique high-flying reconnaissance airplanes built by

Lockheed—the 2,000 mph SR-71 and the 500-mph TR-1—these fly in even duller plumage which is officially a very dark blue, but in fact is indistinguishable from black. There is a reason for all these seemingly unexciting paint schemes. All make airplanes harder to see, and thus harder to shoot down. In the case of the black paint there is a very special additional reason. The paint contains billions of microscopic iron (ferrite) balls, which conduct electricity. When the airplane is caught in an enemy radar the small electric currents flowing through the paint on its surface interfere with the incoming and reflected radar waves and confuse the reflections.

This was the first production application of what is called low-observables, or "stealth," technology. This tries to make tomorrow's warplanes invisible and silent. Of course, total success in such an objective is impossible. It is always possible to detect an airplane visually against its changing backgrounds, while sensitive instruments could hear its noise and detect its heat. But already the US Air Force has two types of Stealth airplane, ahead of any other air force in the world. One is a reconnaissance/strike airplane made by Lockheed. The other is a large intercontinental bomber made by Northrop. These are the only two important new warplanes missing from this book. Even if one could take photographs of them and publish them they would not always show up very clearly, but the reason they are absent from these pages is that in 1988 both airplanes were still highly classified secret.

There is only one defense—
a defense compounded of eternal vigilance,
sound policies, and high courage.

—John Foster Dulles

An F-14A Tomcat of VF-84 "Jolly Rogers," painted in today's toned-down version of their markings, pictured at the moment of firing a radar-guided Sparrow air-to-air missile. This shows how the F-14 looks when its wings are spread out to full span.

Built by McDonnell Aircraft Company at St. Louis, the F-4 Phantom II was the greatest fighter of the Vietnam era.
This is the ultimate model, the F-4E, with an internal 20-millimeter gun under the nose.

After landing most Phantoms are slowed by streaming a drag chute, or "braking parachute,"
along with slats along the wing leading edge and giant flaps at the back of the wing.

A beautiful portrait of an F-4E coming in to land, leaving the sooty trails from its J79 engines characteristic of most Phantoms. Altogether McDonnell built nearly 5,200 Phantoms.

The Aggressor F-5Es are painted in camouflage schemes similar to those used by the Communist Warsaw Pact air forces in Eastern Europe. These are at sunny Edwards AFB in California; another unit, the 527th, is based in rainy England.

Though thousands were sold to friendly nations, the Northrop F-5E, a small twin-jet, served with the US Air Force only in the "Aggressor" role, acting the part of enemy fighters. Here a pair of F-5E Tiger II Aggressors scramble in full afterburner.

Nothing is more exciting than a takeoff in an F-15 Eagle, the USAF's top fighter. At full power
it can climb vertically, straight from takeoff! This F-15 belongs to the Thunderbirds display team.

*Here's another F-15 of the Thunderbirds team, but photographed from a prototype
of the Navy/Marines F-18 Hornet. Both fighters are made by McDonnell Aircraft at St. Louis.*

Diving on its prey like its namesake, this USAF Eagle is fully armed with four AIM-7 Sparrow missiles under the fuselage and four AIM-9 Sidewinder missiles under the wings. It also has a 20-millimeter gun inside the right wing.

Coming in to land, this F-15 will soon transfer its weight to the two small main-gear tires.
And the latest version, the F-15E Strike Eagle, can weigh over 40 tons—as much as 30 to 40 cars!

The white mountains of Utah form a backdrop to this F-16A Fighting Falcon, the newest and—to many pilots—
the most exciting fighter in the US Air Force. Intended as a small "light fighter," it quickly developed into
a brilliantly capable multi-role fighter and attack airplane. The USAF plans to buy no fewer than 2,795.

Compared with the Northrop YF-17, today's Hornet has a much greater fuel capacity, better radar and
the ability to carry heavy loads of bombs and missiles. It is built by McDonnell and Northrop in partnership.

In the air this view of the Hornet prototype shows the high position of the unswept wing, mounted very close to the outward-inclined twin tail fins (vertical stabilizers). Ahead of the wing stretches a long curved "strake" along each side of the fuselage.

The Hornet prototype had NAVY written on one side and MARINES on the other. The black/white striped pole under the engine nozzles is the hinged arrester hook, for landing on aircraft carriers.

Seen from above the prototype Hornet shows its unusual outline. The slightly jagged
leading edge to the wings was made perfectly straight in today's production F/A-18.

This rakish fighter was a prototype of the McDonnell Douglas F/A-18 Hornet, built for the Navy and Marine Corps.
It was developed from the Northrop YF-17, a lightweight fighter built for the Air Force.

A US Air Force general once called the Northrop F-20A Tigershark "The best fighter we never bought."
Developed from the F-5E Tiger II but with many changes, including a single, far more powerful engine, the F-20A was a brilliant performer.

Northrop built three F-20A Tigersharks, and they demonstrated tremendous capability at modest cost. Many airplanes make natural trails of white vapor
from their wingtips, especially during tight maneuvers, but this F-20A was equipped with special smoke generators to heighten the visual effect.

BOMBERS

A view of an FB-111A, taken from the boom-operator's station of a USAF air-refueling tanker.

The long refueling boom can be seen trying to reach down to plug in to the FB's fuel receptacle amidships.

Today only the two final B-52 versions remain in USAF service, the most numerous being the B-52G. About 168 of this model are
active, and they have been subjected to a ceaseless series of structural, systems and above all electronic and weapons improvements.
This G has the twin chin blisters of the EVS (electro-optical viewing system) for low flying at night or in bad weather.
From its open weapon-bay doors could emerge a cruise missile, eight of which can be carried on an internal revolving dispenser.

The F-111 can dump fuel from a pipe between the engine nozzles. Its "party trick" at airshows is to do this while gunning the engines in full afterburner. This is the spectacular result.

As big as a small jetliner, the Fairchild A-10A is a specialized attack airplane intended to destroy targets over a land battle, especially enemy tanks. In the nose can be seen the seven muzzles of its gigantic 30-millimeter gun, the most powerful ever built into an airplane, which can fire up to 70 shells a second, each with a core of depleted uranium to punch through the thickest armor. Under the wings are Maverick missiles and a long electronic-warfare jammer pod.

The cockpit of the A-10A is surrounded by a "bath" of titanium armor a full inch thick— good news for pilots exposed to enemy fire from close range. The A-10A, officially the Thunderbolt II but commonly called the Warthog, is quite a slow airplane, but very well protected and with plenty of lethal punches.

A B-1B thunders out of the test center at Edwards AFB with its four afterburners blazing.

The pivoted swing wings are fully spread, and behind each can be seen the six sections of flap.

Flying low across the sea a B-1B has sinister, serpent-like silhouette. This is the kind of view an enemy might have, but only by chance, because he would be unlikely to have any warning of the bomber's approach.

A B-1B parked with wings fully spread to a span of 136 feet, 8.5 inches. When the wings are swept fully back for high-speed flight, their span is only just over 78 feet. On each side of the nose can be seen the downward-sloping vanes of the SMCS (Structural Mode Control System), which automatically pivot to damp out lateral and vertical shaking of the fuselage when flying through turbulent air at low level.

The B-1B's fuselage and wing blend smoothly into each other. Where they do so the interior is packed with high-power electronics to help defeat enemy defense systems and protect the bomber against any kind of interception.

The B-1's crew of four have to know how to get up this ladder fast, because in an emergency they might have to be scrambled before missiles fell on their airbase. The first B-1B base is Dyess AFB, near Abilene, Texas. By mid-1988 SAC will have 100 B-1Bs.

This amazing picture was taken from under the fuselage of a Lockheed TR-1 parked on the flight line (another is in the distance). The camera was pointed out along beneath the wing. At the left can be seen the two sections of flap, in the "down" position. Near the far end is the small outrigger gear with twin wheels, which stops the aircraft from rolling on to a wingtip. On takeoff both these outrigger gears are jettisoned. On landing, the TR-1 does roll on to a wingtip.

On operational missions a TR-1A would carry giant payload pods about one-third of the way along its wings. Without them, as here, the high-flying Lockheed looks almost exactly like the notorious U-2 (shot down over Sverdlovsk on 1 May 1960) from which it was developed.

First flown back in 1954, the Cessna T-37B was the first USAF jet trainer. About 600 are still in use. A plan to replace these with the new Fairchild T-46A was cancelled in 1986, so the aging "Tweets" (as they are called) will have to go on training the Air Force's pilots for a long time. Instructor and pupil sit side by side.

The white-painted Northrop T-38 Talon is an unusual airplane, in that it is a supersonic trainer, yet over the past 27 years almost every USAF combat pilot got his advanced training in it. The immediate ancestor of the F-5 fighter, about 900 remain in use.

What are the most vital support airplanes? All are needed, but none more than the GD/Grumman EF-111A Raven EW (Electronic Warfare) airplanes. Rebuilt by Grumman from former F-111A attack bombers, the EFs are packed with electronic devices that listen for hostile radar and radio emissions, check their exact wavelength and other characteristics, and then jam them so that other US airplanes can fly attack missions with less chance of being shot down. Most of the receivers are on top of the tail, and the jammers are along the belly.

This is the view that an enemy fighter pilot would like to get of a TR-1, if he could climb high enough. In wartime the TR-1 would probably stay on its own side of a hostile frontier or battlefront, but would "see" in great detail a distance of about 35 miles into enemy territory using a SLAR (sideways-looking airborne radar).

Somewhere over the (probably Western) United States a black TR-1A slips almost silently through the stratosphere. It is not carrying mission pods, but on the wingtips can be seen the small circular golden antennas, facing outward fore and aft, of the RHAW (radar homing and warning) system. This helps to protect against being shot down.

Like the black SR-71, the TR-1 was designed by Lockheed-California Company at its secret "Skunk Works," which has an amazing record of creating advanced airplanes without any publicity. The TR-1 is also painted in anti-radar black, and it looks down into foreign territories from heights between 70,000 and (it is said) 90,000 feet. To fly so high it has amazing glider-like wings, with a span of 103 feet.

Among the most costly aircraft in any air force, the USAF's E-3A Sentry AWACS (Airborne Warning And Control System) airplanes are based on the airframe of the Boeing 707 jetliner. Westinghouse developed the powerful radar, which uses a giant antenna slowly rotating high above the fuselage to sweep its beam round through 360° once every ten seconds. Complex displays in front of (typically) 16 AWACS mission specialists provide information on all activity out to a radius of 230 miles. This E-3A has just taken off.

In the introduction it was stated that the Lockheed "stealth" reconnaissance strike airplane (sometimes mistakenly believed to be a fighter, the "F-19") would not be found in this book. That is true, but this picture is one of many that claim to be of this mysterious aircraft. It is probably not a bad likeness, but we shall have to wait and see.

Made like the C-130 at Lockheed-Georgia Company, the C-141 Starlifter is about the size of a 707 or DC-8 but has less sweep on a high-mounted wing. It thus flies rather slower, but carries more and needs shorter runways. Lockheed built 284 white-painted C-141As, but today all the survivors have been stretched by 23 feet 4 inches to turn them into more capacious C-141Bs, a further improvement being the bulge above the forward fuselage which houses a flight-refueling receptacle. Today the C-141Bs are painted in Europe 1 camouflage.

A special version of the Lockheed Hercules is the KC-130, used in several sub-versions by the Marine Corps. The prefix "K" means it can serve as an air-refueling tanker. Under the outer wings are British-style hose-drum units from which fuel hoses fitted with conical drogues can be unreeled. Here two big CH-53E helicopters have thrust in their probes to take on fuel.

Nobody could win a war without a lot of transport, and by far the most numerous transport airplane in the US inventory is the Lockheed C-130 Hercules. Popularly called the "Herky-bird," this tough and versatile machine, powered by four 4,500-horsepower Allison turboprops, has been in production at Marietta, Georgia, since 1955. Here paratroops are jumping from the right-hand rear door.

The USAF air-refueling tankers mostly use the Boeing-developed rigid Flying Boom technique. The receiver has to formate very accurately below and behind the tanker while a boom operator in the tanker "flies" his boom until he can extend it with a fuel-tight joint into the receiver receptacle. Here a Boeing KC-135 refuels a prototype Cessna AT-37, while an F-4 takes photos (because this was a test run).

With a long-focus lens it was possible to capture this dramatic shot of an SR-71A in full afterburner crossing the full moon. Even today many of the advanced camera and other reconnaissance sensors carried by these fantastic airplanes are highly classified.

If there were an Old Man in the Moon he would be impressed by the loads that can be put aboard the vast Lockheed C-5 Galaxy through its gaping maw. "Maw" is a pun, because they all serve with MAWs—USAF Military Airlift Wings—and today these white-painted C-5As have been supplemented by 50 completely new C-5Bs, all painted in dark camouflage. The Galaxy is as big as a 747 jumbo jet, though its engines are rather less powerful at 43,000 pounds of thrust each.

The term "support aircraft" certainly could include the experimental and research airplanes that help the development of the next generation of warplanes. Few aircraft are as striking in appearance as the Grumman X-29, the first ever to explore the advantages of the FSW (forward-swept wing). As the horizontal control surface is in front of the wing it looks as if the plane was built back-to-front, but in fact (assisted by computers) the X-29 flies like a dream.

A Grumman engineering test pilot shuts the canopy prior to another test mission with one of the two X-29s. The amazing FSW is stiffened with diagonal plies (layers) of strong carbon fiber. Any traditional FSW would simply be torn off in high-speed maneuvers.

HELICOPTERS

Though it was directly developed from the familiar "Huey," the Bell AH-1 HueyCobra—popularly called the Snake—looks utterly different, because instead of a wide cabin it has a pair of tandem cockpits like a fighter. In front sits the gunner, who manages the weapons (which in this twin-engined SeaCobra of the Marine Corps includes a powerful three-barrel cannon). Behind and at a higher level sits the pilot, who can throw the 'Cobra around like a fighter.

This is a familiar silhouette to thousands of American helicopter pilots. Made by Bell Helicopter Textron, at Fort Worth, Texas, the UH-1— officially the Iroquois, but universally known as the "Huey"—has been made in larger numbers than any non-Soviet aircraft since World War II. First flown in 1956, it was by far the most numerous helicopter in Vietnam, and hundreds still serve with the Army, Navy, Air Force and Marines. Most have 1,100 horsepower and can carry ten passengers.

In the McDonnell Douglas AH-64A Apache the US Army is sure it has the best-armed battlefield helicopter in the world. Powered by slightly more powerful versions of the same engine as in the Black Hawk, the Apache has tandem cockpits for pilot and gunner and very comprehensive electronic vision and aiming systems for operations at low level at night or in bad weather. Under the wings 16 Hellfire missiles (or other weapons) can be hung, while under the nose is a hard-hitting 30-millimeter gun.

Sikorsky pioneered the idea of a crane helicopter with these CH-54 Tarhe helicopters of the US Army. Powered by two 4,800-horsepower engines, the CH-54 has no fuselage—just a cockpit at the nose and a strong girder linking the other parts together. It straddles its load and carries it slung externally. Maximum load is ten tons.

Here seen thundering over the California desert during an assault exercise, the Sikorsky CH-53E Super Stallion is the most powerful American helicopter, with three General Electric engines of 4,380 horsepower each, driving a huge, seven-blade rotor. With the landing gears retracted these massive machines can almost reach 200 mph, even with 55 troops on board. Note the big drop tanks slung under the stub wings.

Two of the most famous helicopters are here seen flying together. The Bell UH-1 "Huey" is on the left, while on the right is the Sikorsky CH-3E, the special transport version of the Navy's SH-3 Sea King anti-submarine helicopter. Powered by two 1,500-horsepower T58 engines, the CH-3E is closely related to the HH-3E Jolly Green Giant, which was the rescue helo in Vietnam.

In this head-on view the Army AH-1S Cobra shows off its narrow fuselage, angular canopy and deadly array of rockets and missile launchers under the short wings. The thing looking like a dart held out beside the cockpit is a local airstream director, which helps in aiming the weapons.

FORMATION TEAMS

Famed the world over, the USAF's premier
formation display team is The Thunderbirds.
This photo was taken when they flew
the slim Northrop T-38 Talon supersonic trainer.

Today the Thunderbirds fly the powerful General
Dynamics F-16 Fighting Falcon. Most F-16s are
powered by a single Pratt & Whitney F100 engine of
23,450 pounds of thrust, enough for really impressive
maneuvers in the vertical as well as the horizontal
plane. The smoke is deliberate.

It's the Fourth of July 1986, and here are America's two top formation display teams together. In front, the Navy's Blue Angels; just to the left, the USAF's Thunderbirds, proudly showing off their new F-16s.

A top formation display team is "on parade" the whole time it is in front of the public, not just while it is in the air. This is how the Navy's Blue Angels look as they taxi out to begin a display.

Here seen just coming in over the stern of a carrier, the Vought (LTV) A-7 Corsair II was developed with extreme rapidity by a design team at Dallas in 1964-65. It was planned to replace the A-4 Skyhawk; though the A-4 stayed in production, the A-7 proved a great success, carrying heavy attack loads over long ranges and delivering with great accuracy. This is an A-7E, with the outstanding TF41 engine and upgraded electronic systems.

Unquestionably the top plane in the Navy is the Grumman F-14 Tomcat, perhaps the world's best-armed fighter and the only airplane to carry not only Sparrow and Sidewinder missiles but also the great Phoenix, which can knock down an enemy airplane from a range of over 100 miles. Here an F-14A comes up on the elevator along with loads of bombs for attack airplanes.

An F-14A of the "Jolly Rogers" squadron goes down on the deck-edge elevator to the level of the hangar. This sometimes has to be done with the ship heaving in a storm. Note the folded-wing Hawkeye radar plane on deck.

A varied assortment of aircraft can be seen parked on the deck of this carrier—probably CV-63 Kitty Hawk—during the Vietnam era. In the bows are piston-engined A-1 Skyraiders, A-4 Skyhawks and A-7 Corsair IIs. Further back are big A-3 Skywarrior attack bombers and E-1 Tracer radar early-warning planes.

Today the F-14s are plain gray all over, but previously they were boldly painted in unit markings. This F-14A from Navy Squadron VF-84, "The Jolly Rogers," was typical. The "Jolly Roger" was the famed pirate flag, painted on the tail.

An F-14A of Squadron VF-84 aboard Nimitz, *with its wings fully swept back. The F-14 has two Pratt & Whitney engines, a crew of two, a powerful radar, masses of weapons and can do practically anything—its crews will tell you.*

Coming in over the stern of Nimitz, *and a few seconds from picking up a wire, this Lockheed S-3A Viking represents the very latest in carrier-based ASW (anti-submarine warfare) aircraft—and also an amazing exercise in packaging. In a small package, which folds to fit a cramped carrier hangar, Lockheed shoehorned a crew of four with ejection seats in an air-conditioned cockpit, two turbofan engines and fuel for 3,000 miles, radar, infrared, sonobuoys, a magnetic-anomaly detector (for finding submerged submarines), complex electronic-warfare systems and, not least, a heavy load of torpedoes, bombs, depth bombs or anti-ship cruise missiles!*

The Navy has 72 unarmed Grumman KA-6D Intruders, which were built as attack airplanes but converted into air refueling tankers. Here seen parked with its wings folded and with four drop tanks to increase the fuel load, the KA-6D has a British-style hose-drum unit in the rear fuselage through which it can transfer over 21,000 pounds of fuel.

To provide quick transport between the nearest friendly port and the carrier—of visitors, urgent supplies and all sorts of other items—the Navy uses COD (Carrier On-board Delivery) aircraft. Today's COD is the C-2A Greyhound, derived from the Hawkeye, but this picture shows its predecessor, the Grumman C-1A Trader. COD airplanes have to fold (as shown), and be strong enough to make catapult launches and arrested landings.

An F-14 costs at least $30 million, but thin steel cables make sure this one cannot roll off the edge of the deck. Today Grumman is delivering the upgraded F-14A Plus and F-14D, with much more powerful General Electric F110 engines and new electronics.

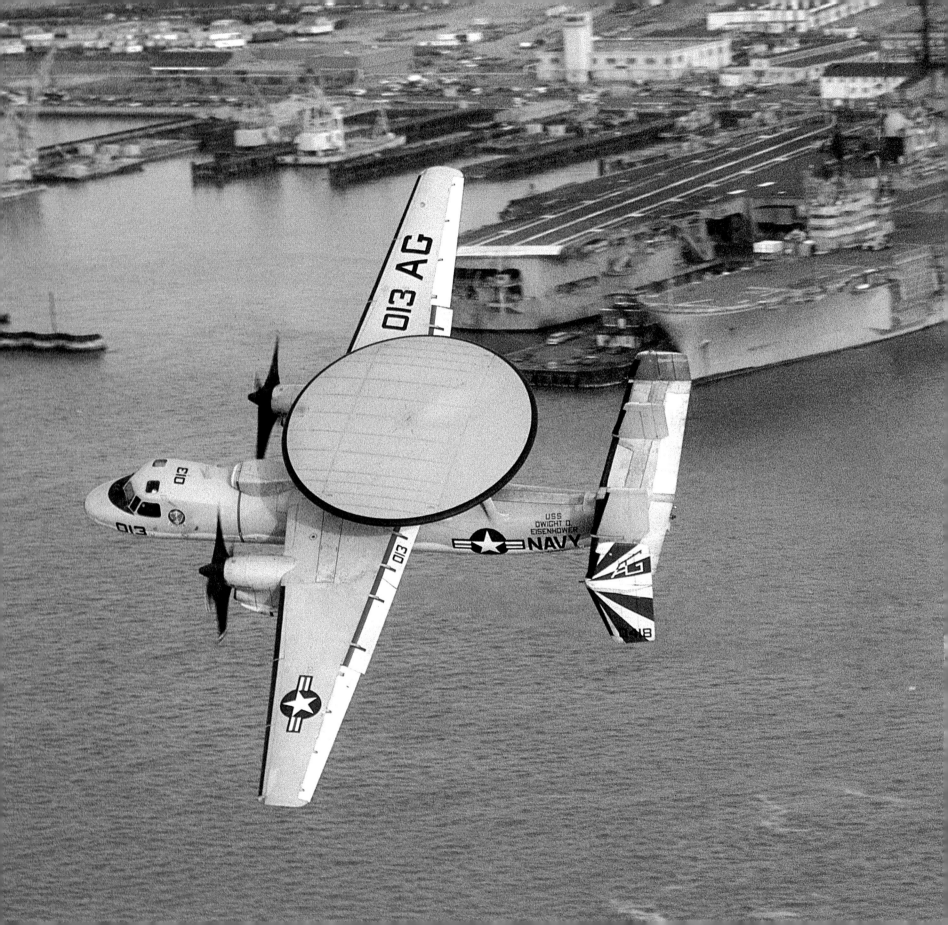

McDonnell Douglas F-4E Phantom II

• Two-seat all-weather fighter
• Two General Electric J79-17 turbojets of maximum thrust of 17,900 pounds each (with afterburner)
• Span 38 ft 5 in; length 63 ft
• Maximum loaded weight 60,360 pounds
• Maximum speed at high altitude 1,500 mph (Mach 2.27)
• Armament: One 20-mm M61 gun, and up to 16,000 pounds of bombs, rockets or other attack stores, or four AIM-7 Sparrow AAMs (air-to-air missiles) and four AIM-9 Sidewinder AAMs.

Northrop F-5E Tiger II

• Single-seat day fighter
• Two General Electric J85-21A turbojets of maximum thrust of 5,000 pounds each (with afterburner)
• Span (including tip AAMs) 27 ft 11 in; length 48 ft 2 in
• Maximum loaded weight 24,676 pounds
• Maximum speed at high altitude 1,077 mph (Mach 1.63)
• Armament: Two M39A2 20-mm guns, plus up to 7,000 pounds of attack weapons including two AIM-9 Sidewinder AAMs on the wingtips.

Though all it does is cruise gently about at a height of some 30,000 feet, many people on a giant carrier would say the Grumman E-2C Hawkeye is the most important airplane aboard. Its powerful radar sweeps round to all points of the compass, unfailingly detecting the approach of hostile aircraft or ships out to a radius of almost 300 miles. The Hawkeye can warn the fleet, direct friendly fighters to intercept, direct attack aircraft to enemy ships and in many other ways multiply the effectiveness of the Carrier Air Wing.

Grumman F-14A Tomcat

- Two-seat all-weather carrier-based interceptor
- Two Pratt & Whitney TF30-414A turbofans of maximum thrust of 20,900 pounds each (with afterburner)
- Span (wings fully swept back) 38 ft 2 in, (wings fully spread) 64 ft 1.5 in; length 62 ft 8 in
- Maximum loaded weight 74,348 pounds
- Maximum speed at high altitude 1,544 mph (Mach 2.34)
- Armament: One 20-mm M61 gun, and many AAM combinations such as: six AIM-54 Phoenix and two AIM-9 Sidewinder; or four AIM-7 Sparrow and four or eight AIM-9 Sidewinder. In the attack mission (rare) a 14,500-pound weapon load can be carried.

McDonnell Douglas F-15C Eagle

- Single-seat all-weather fighter
- Two Pratt & Whitney F100-100 turbofans of maximum thrust of 23,930 pounds each (with afterburner)
- Span 42 ft 9.75 in; length 63 ft 9 in
- Maximum loaded weight 68,000 pounds
- Maximum speed at high altitude 1,650 mph (Mach 2.5)
- Armament: One 20-mm M61 gun, and either four AIM-7 Sparrow AAMs plus four AIM-9 Sidewinder AAMs or (from late 1988) up to eight AIM-120A AMRAAM missiles
- Note: The F-15E is a two-seat dual-role version able to carry a weapon load of 23,500 pounds, the loaded weight then being 81,000 pounds.

General Dynamics F-16C Fighting Falcon

- Single-seat all-weather multirole fighter/bomber
- One Pratt & Whitney F100-220 turbofan (23,450 pounds) or one General Electric F110-100 turbofan (27,600 pounds), in each case the thrust being the maximum with afterburner
- Span (including tip AAMs) 32 ft 10 in; length 49 ft 3 in
- Maximum loaded weight 37,500 pounds
- Maximum speed at high altitude 1,320 mph (Mach 2.0)
- Armament: One 20-mm M61 gun, plus up to 12,000 pounds of ordnance such as bombs, rockets, air-to-ground missiles, anti-ship missiles or a variety of AAMs.

McDonnell Douglas F/A-18A Hornet

- Single-seat carrier-based all-weather fighter and attack aircraft
- Two General Electric F404-400 turbofans of maximum thrust of 16,000 pounds each (with afterburner)
- Span (including tip AAMs) 40 ft 4.75 in; length 56 ft 0 in
- Maximum loaded weight 49,224 pounds
- Maximum speed at high altitude 1,188 mph (Mach 1.8)
- Armament: One 20-mm M61 gun, and up to 17,000 pounds of external weapons including AIM-7 Sparrow, AIM-9 Sidewinder or AIM-120A AMRAAM AAMs, Harpoon anti-ship missiles, bombs or rockets.

General Dynamics FB-111A

- Two-seat all-weather low-level bomber
- Two Pratt & Whitney TF30-7 turbofans of maximum thrust of 20,350 pounds each (with afterburner)
- Span (wings fully swept back) 33 ft 11 in, (fully spread) 70 ft 0 in
- Maximum loaded weight 114,300 pounds
- Maximum speed at high altitude 1,320 mph (Mach 2.0)
- Armament: Internal stowage for up to two SRAM missiles, plus up to four more carried externally; alternatively a theoretical capability of carrying 41,250 pounds of conventional HE bombs.

Boeing B52-G Stratofortress

- Heavy bomber
- Eight Pratt & Whitney J57-43WB turbojets each of maximum thrust of 13,750 pounds
- Span 185 ft 0 in; length 160 ft 11 in
- Maximum loaded weight 505,000 pounds
- Maximum speed at high altitude 595 mph
- Armament: Up to eight SRAM missiles carried internally, plus up to 12 SRAM or ALCM (cruise) missiles carried externally, or Harpoon anti-ship missiles, or varying loads of nuclear or conventional free-fall bombs; four 0.5-in guns in defensive tail turret.

Rockwell B-1B

- Strategic bomber and missile platform
- Four General Electric F101-102 turbofans of maximum thrust of "30,000-pounds class" (with afterburner)
- Span (wings fully swept back) 78 ft 2.5 in, (fully spread) 136 ft 8.5 in; length 147 ft 0 in
- Maximum loaded weight 477,000 pounds
- Maximum speed at high altitude about 825 mph (Mach 1.25)
- Armament: Internal and external stowage for up to 22 ALCM cruise missiles, 38 SRAM attack missiles, many nuclear bombs (for example, 38 B61 or B83 free-fall bombs) or 128 Mk 82 conventional HE bombs.

Fairchild A-10A Thunderbolt II

- Single-seat close-support and anti-tank aircraft
- Two General Electric TF34-100 turbofans of maximum thrust of 9,065 pounds each
- Span 57 ft 6 in; length 53 ft 4 in
- Maximum loaded weight 50,000 pounds
- Maximum speed at sea level 423 mph
- Armament: One 30-mm GAU-8/A gun with armor-piercing ammunition, plus up to 14,638 pounds of bombs, Maverick air/ground missiles, rockets or other stores, with full internal fuel.

Grumman A-6E Intruder

- Two-seat carrier-based all-weather attack aircraft
- Two Pratt & Whitney J52-8A turbojets of maximum thrust of 9,300 pounds each
- Span 53 ft 0 in; length 54 ft 7 in
- Maximum loaded weight 60,400 pounds
- Maximum speed at sea level (higher than at altitude) 684 mph
- Armament: Up to 15,000 pounds of bombs or other offensive stores carried on five external pylons each rated at 3,600 pounds (typical load, 30 bombs of 500 pounds).

Vought A-7E Corsair II

- Single-seat (almost all-weather) carrier-based attack aircraft
- One Allison/Rolls-Royce TF41-2 turbofan of maximum thrust of 15,000 pounds
- Span 38 ft 9 in; length 46 ft 1.5 in
- Maximum loaded weight 42,000 pounds
- Maximum speed at sea level 698 mph
- Armament: One 20-mm M61 gun, plus up to a theoretical maximum load of 20,000 pounds of bombs, missiles, rockets or other ordnance, with self-defense AIM-9 Sidewinder AAMs carried on the sides of the fuselage.

Bell AH-1S HueyCobra

- Two-seat close-support and attack helicopter
- One 1,800-horsepower Avco Lycoming T53-703 turboshafts
- Main-rotor diameter 44 ft 0 in; overall length (including rotors) 52 ft 11.5 in
- Maximum loaded weight 10,000 pounds
- Maximum speed at sea level 141 mph (with TOW missiles)
- Armament: Chin turret with either one 7.62-mm gun and one 40mm grenade launcher or (current) one 20-mm M197 gun; anti-tank weapons can comprise up to eight TOW missiles, plus up to four launchers each firing 7 or 19 rockets of 2.75-in caliber.

McDonnell Douglas AH-64A Apache

- Two-seat all-weather attack helicopter
- Two General Electric 1,696-horsepower T700-701 turboshafts
- Main-rotor diameter 48 ft 0 in; overall length (including rotors) 58 ft 3.2 in
- Maximum loaded weight: 21,000 pounds
- Maximum speed at sea level 184 mph
- Armament: One 30-mm M230 gun, plus up to 16 Hellfire advanced anti-tank guided missiles, or up to 76 rockets of 2.75-in caliber.

INDEX OF PHOTOGRAPHERS